CONTENTS

Mike the pilot

My name is Mike.

I am an airline pilot.

Today I am going to fly a plane
from London to New York.

New York

London

N

W E

S

Let's look at the plane

I am going to fly a jumbo jet.

I sit in the cockpit.

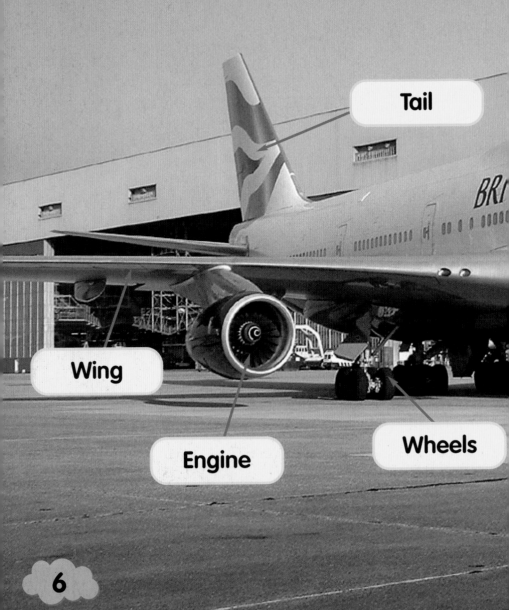

Tail

Wing

Engine

Wheels

Cockpit

Windows

Door

A jumbo jet has 188 windows and 18 wheels.

Checking the plane

I must check the plane.

I check the wheels.

I check the lights.

I check under the plane.

Everything looks OK.

Wheels

In the cockpit

There are two pilots.

I am the captain.

Don is the co-pilot.

He will help me fly the plane.

I check the controls in the cockpit.

Controls

I check the weather.

Sunny   Rainy   Stormy   Snowy

Don checks the map.

Map

Take-off

We have checked everything is OK.

We are ready for take-off.

Runway

The plane goes down the runway.

It gets faster and faster.

Then it takes off.

Wheels

The wheels go up into the plane.

Flying to America

The plane flies at 570 miles per hour.

There are 412 passengers on the plane.

The flight attendants give the passengers food and drinks.

The passengers watch a film.

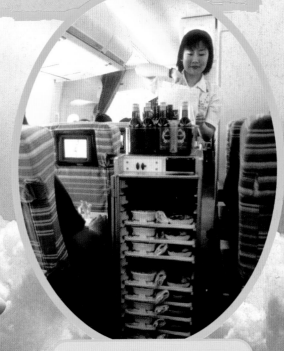

Flight attendant

Pilots at work

We are working.

Don checks the weather and the fuel.

I check how fast the plane is going.

It takes six hours to fly to New York.

Airline food

We eat and drink in the cockpit.

Landing

Can I land in New York?

I must ask air traffic control.

Air traffic control

They check the weather.

They check the runway.

Air traffic control say I can land.

The wheels come down again.

Welcome to New York

I land the plane in New York.

The passengers get
off the plane.

Runway

It was a good flight.

I am happy.

Passengers

Wheels

Yes or no? Talking about pilots and planes

There are two pilots.

Yes or no?

The jumbo jet has 18 windows.

Yes or no?

Mike and Don eat in the cockpit.

Yes or no?

The plane lands in London.

Yes or no?

Would you like to be a pilot?
Why or why not?

Activities

What did you think of this book?

 Brilliant **Good** **OK**

Which page did you like best? Why?

• • • • • • • • • • • • •

Which is the odd one out? Why?

engines • lights • map • wheels

• • • • • • • • • • • • •

Draw a big picture of a jumbo jet and label it. Use these words:

cockpit • door • engine • window • wing

• • • • • • • • • • • • •

Who is the author of this book?
Have you read *Animal Hospital* by the same author?